hro

probably no scriptural passage that is read more frequently or more widely than Luke chapter two, which begins, "And it came to pass in those days, that there went out a decree from Caesar Augustus, that all the world should be taxed." (Luke 2:1.)

This chapter and the related passages in the first chapter of Luke and the first two chapters of Matthew contain what we call the Christmas story. It is a story beloved by millions and read in a myriad of languages each December. That story has inspired plays, musicals, short fiction, novels, and pageants. As recorded by Matthew and Luke, the account is simple and straight-forward. Over the centuries many additions have been made, and numerous embellishments have crept in. Were there three wise men, and do we know their names? Was the innkeeper an insensitive lout who turned away a woman in travail? Does the traditional Christmas crèche with its wooden stable and the shepherds and wise men standing all together around the manger really reflect what it was like on that night of nights?

There is much of interest that we know about the culture and traditions of that day when Mary and Joseph went to Bethlehem. Without resorting to legend or unsubstantiated embellishment, we can still find much that will enrich our understanding of the events that ushered in the most sacred of Christian holy days. With that greater understanding, we can read the Christmas story with deeper appreciation—which will add to our profound gratitude for the coming of Jesus Christ into the world some two thousand years ago.

"The Birth of Jesus Christ Was on This Wise"

"And in the sixth month the angel Gabriel was sent from God unto a city of Galilee, named Nazareth." (Luke 1:26.)

The rabbis of ancient Israel had a saying: "Judea is wheat, Galilee straw, and beyond Jordan, only chaff."[1] The urbane and worldly wise Jerusalemites, privileged to dwell in the Holy City, looked down on all others with condescension; but they especially viewed the Galileans as crude, unlearned, and earthy peasants. For the most part, the people of Galilee were men and women of the soil and of the sea. This kept them in touch with basic values; and in spite of the feelings of the Judeans, they were known for being hardworking and warmhearted, and for showing unrestrained hospitality and uncompromising honesty.

As for Nazareth itself, like many other villages of Judea and Galilee, it sat amid steep, tree-covered hillsides so as not to utilize precious agricultural land. For a village now so famous, it seems to have been of singular insignificance then. It is not even mentioned in the Old Testament or in the extensive writings of the ancient historian Josephus. Nathanael expressed what must have been a common feeling even among the Galileans when he said, "Can there any good thing come out of Nazareth?" (John 1:46.) Evidently, the suggestion that the Messiah had come from such a civic backwater was unthinkable.

ENGAGEMENT OF JOSEPH AND MARY

"To a virgin espoused to a man whose name was Joseph, of the house of David." (Luke 1:27.)

As we are dropped into the midst of their lives, Joseph and Mary are "espoused." (Matthew 1:18.) Espousal—meaning engagement, not marriage—among the Hebrews was significantly more binding than are our engagements today. The couple entered into it by written agreement and considered it the formal beginning of the marriage itself. While the couple did not actually live together for as long as a year after the betrothal—a time designed for the bride to prepare her dowry—the espousal was as legally binding as the formal marriage.

The scriptural text gives no hint of the age of either Mary or Joseph, but from existing sources we can make some educated guesses. We know that puberty began somewhat earlier in the ancient Middle East than is common in Western countries today. Therefore, marriage at earlier ages than we are accustomed to was the general rule. Speaking of the typical man, one rabbi described the stages of development as follows: At five he began study of Torah; at ten, study of the Mishnah (the oral laws); at fifteen, the study of Talmud (the extensive commentaries on the scriptures). At eighteen he married; and at twenty he pursued a trade or business.[2] For a girl, probably the most common age of marriage was fifteen or sixteen. Sometimes it was later, sometimes earlier, but it is likely that Mary was around sixteen, and Joseph, her espoused husband, only two or three years older.

Nazareth was a small village. Joseph and Mary must have known each other well. How fascinating it would be to know the circumstances that brought them to the point of betrothal. Much is made of the fact that in those days families arranged marriages through the auspices of a matchmaker. No doubt that was true, but that does not mean the individuals involved had no voice in the matter. We know from contemporary sources that, once the arrangements were made, the consent of the couple was required. The man had a direct say in the choice of his bride, and the woman could refuse the marital arrangements if they were not to her satisfaction.[3] So what was it that drew these two together?

We know that Mary must have been of unusual loveliness. Nephi saw her in vision some six hundred years before her birth and described her as "exceedingly fair" and "most beautiful and fair." (1 Nephi 11:13, 15.) But did Joseph see only the outward beauty, or did he sense the same qualities that caused Gabriel to declare that this woman was "highly favoured" of the Lord? (Luke 1:28.) No wonder Joseph loved her! Imagine finding a woman of such remarkable grace and beauty in a small village in the mountains of Galilee.

And what of Joseph? What was it about this man that caused Mary to give her consent to the marriage arrangements? Only a few scriptural verses tell us about Joseph. He was a carpenter, that we know. (See Matthew 13:55.) And because fathers commonly taught their sons their own trade, Joseph was likely reared in a carpenter's shop. His hands would have been rough and calloused. He was a man of labor, a man who created things through his own craftsmanship.

Matthew also describes him as a "just man." (Matthew 1:19.) It is a simple phrase, yet it speaks volumes, for those same words are used to describe such men as Noah, Job, Nephi, and Jacob. Was it purely by accident that such a man was in Nazareth waiting to be Mary's partner in this most significant of dramas? Surely God the Father had seen in Joseph a man worthy to raise His Son and help prepare Him for His mortal ministry. While it would not be Joseph's privilege to actually father the "Firstborn," it would be his labor that would provide for His needs, his voice that would encourage His first steps, his hands that would guide His fingers across the sacred scrolls of the Torah in those first Hebrew lessons. Joseph was also the one who would put a mallet and chisel and plane in those smaller hands so that one day this boy from Nazareth would also be known as "the carpenter." (Mark 6:3.) No wonder Mary loved him!

THE NAME MARY

"And the virgin's name was Mary." (Luke 1:27.)

One of the most common feminine names in the New Testament is Mary—Miryam (Miriam) in Hebrew. One Bible concordance identifies at least seven different Marys in the New Testament, so it is not surprising to find a virgin of that name in the village of Nazareth.[4] But perhaps there is more to it than that. Among Book of Mormon prophets, even a hundred years before the birth of the Savior, the actual name of the woman who was to mother the Messiah was known. (See Mosiah 3:8; Alma 7:10.) If that was so among Book of Mormon prophets, is it not possible that the significance of the name was also known among Old Testament prophets as well, and therefore among the people of the Holy Land?

We know from existing records that the people at the time of Christ's birth generally believed that the birth of the long-awaited Messiah was imminent. What mother would not hope that her daughter might be the promised vessel for such an honor? Such maternal optimism might explain the frequency with which daughters were named Mary. But for whatever reason, Mary's mother fulfilled prophetic promises when she named her child, her little daughter who would be the one to become the chosen vessel of the Lord.

GABRIEL'S SALUTATION

"And the angel came in unto her, and said, Hail, thou that art highly favoured, the Lord is with thee: blessed art thou among women. And when she saw him, she was troubled at his saying, and cast in her mind what manner of salutation this should be. And the angel said unto her, Fear not, Mary: for thou hast found favour with God. And, behold, thou shalt conceive in thy womb, and bring forth a son, and shalt call his name JESUS." (Luke 1:28–31.)

It was early July in Galilee.[5] The heat, even at night, can be stifling and oppressive. Luke indicates that Mary and Joseph were likely of poor families.[6] If that was the case, the house of Mary's family would have been small, no more than one or two rooms curtained off for sleeping and privacy at night.

We are not told if it was day or night, or if she was alone in the house or out of doors, but surely she must have felt a sudden clutch of fear when she looked up and saw a personage standing before her. All of us have had someone come up behind us or appear in a doorway unexpectedly and startle us. We give an involuntary cry of surprise and feel the quick burst of adrenaline that leaves the heart pounding, the palms sweaty, and the mouth dry. So it is not difficult to imagine the shock of having not just a man, but a being of transcendent radiance and glory, appear suddenly in your room.

But the shock of Gabriel's sudden appearance could not have been any greater than the stunning impact of his words. First there was the "impossible" announcement that she was about to conceive. Her response is so spontaneous, so logical. It adds even further to the power and simplicity with which Luke tells us of this night. One can almost picture her blurting it out, in spite of the glory of the being standing before her: "How shall this be, seeing I know not a man?" (Luke 1:34.)

But that was only the first of the stunning pronouncements. The Messiah had been foretold for four millennia. Now to realize that the long centuries of waiting had come to an end, that the Messiah was about to be born, and that she—Mary of Nazareth—was to be the mother! Add to that the declaration that, for the first and only time in the history of the world, this was to be a virgin birth, and the revelation was even more staggering. This simple, pure woman from a little-known city in Galilee was to carry in her womb the divine offspring of the great Elohim Himself. Her son would be the Son of God!

Only when we consider the magnitude of Gabriel's statements do we begin to appreciate how marvelous Mary's answer is. There were no questioning looks, no stammering demands of "Why me?"

There were no murmurs of doubt. There was no disputation, no hesitation, no wondering. In glorious and touching simplicity, she said: "Behold the handmaid of the Lord; be it unto me according to thy word." (Luke 1:38.)

MARY'S PREGNANCY

"Now the birth of Jesus Christ was on this wise: When as his mother Mary was espoused to Joseph, before they came together, she was found with child of the Holy Ghost." (Matthew 1:18.)

After Gabriel's announcement, Mary left Nazareth to visit her cousin Elisabeth, wife of Zacharias the priest, living in Judea. Elisabeth was six months pregnant with a miracle of her own, and Mary abode with her kinswoman about three months until the time came for Elisabeth to deliver.

Consider for a moment what coming back to Nazareth at that point must have meant for Mary. She had suddenly, unexpectedly departed from her home for an extended stay far to the south. When she returned, the growing child within the womb was expanding to swell her belly. It was not a secret that could be hidden for long.

This was not a society like our own where immorality is not only tolerated but often openly flaunted. Modesty and virtue were deeply ingrained into the fiber of the nation and were especially strong in the small towns and villages of Israel. Imagine the effect on that tiny village when Mary returned and the first of the village women began to notice the change in her.

Anyone who has ever lived in the tightly knit, closely bonded society of a small town or village can predict with some accuracy what happened next. At first there may have been only questioning looks and quick shakings of the head. Surely it could not be so. Not Mary. Perhaps she was just putting on a little weight. Then more and more voices would have questioned—not openly, of course, but in whispers, at the well each day as they came together for water or while doing the laundry on the banks of a stream.

Was Mary allowed to tell others of her visit from Gabriel? Matthew's comment "she was *found* with child" would imply that she was not. (Emphasis added.) But even if she were allowed to tell, would such a seemingly fantastic claim have quelled the rumors? A virgin birth? Mother of the Messiah? A child fathered by God Himself? Either she was mad, or she took them for absolute fools to imagine they would believe such a story. To the villagers, her departure from the village "with haste" probably took on new and ominous significance. (See Luke 1:39.) And poor Joseph. Victim of such "infidelity." What would he do now?

JOSEPH TAKES MARY TO WIFE

"Then Joseph her husband, being a just man, and not willing to make her a publick example, was minded to put her away privily. But while he thought on these things, behold, the angel of the Lord appeared unto him in a dream, saying, Joseph, thou son of David, fear not to take unto thee Mary thy wife: for that which is conceived in her is of the Holy Ghost…. Then Joseph being raised from sleep did as the angel of the Lord had bidden him, and took unto him his wife." (Matthew 1:19–20, 24.)

Neither Luke nor Matthew gives us much detail, but we can read the hurt and embarrassment between the lines. Here was a good man, faithful in every respect. What pain must have filled his soul to learn that his betrothed was with child! Surely not Mary, not his lovely and chaste Mary. We can only guess at the agony of spirit he must have experienced at the seeming confirmation of her "unfaithfulness."

How many men would let the bitterness and anger of such betrayal fester and then boil over into a blind desire to strike out in revenge, seeking to hurt as deeply as they themselves are hurt? Besides, by Mosaic law, adultery was punishable by death. (See, for example, John 8:4–5; Leviticus 20:10.) Joseph could have taken Mary to the elders of the village and demanded justice. But, despite the pain he must have felt, despite the personal humiliation, he would not put his beloved Mary through the shame and danger of a public trial. He would simply dissolve the marriage contract quietly.

But then, in one blinding instant of revelation, all was explained and put right. In response to Gabriel's incredible announcement, Mary had simply said, "Behold the handmaid of the Lord." Now Joseph heard a similar stunning announcement. We gain a glimpse of the greatness of the man from his response. Matthew says it in one phrase: "Then Joseph *being raised from sleep* . . . took unto him his wife." (Matthew 1:24; emphasis added.) The phrase suggests that little time elapsed between the announcement and the marriage, perhaps with it even occurring before dawn.

THE TOWN CALLED BETHLEHEM

"And it came to pass in those days, that there went out a decree from Caesar Augustus, that all the world should be taxed. . . . And all went to be taxed, every one into his own city. And Joseph also went up from Galilee, out of the city of Nazareth, into Judaea, unto the city of David, which is called Bethlehem; (because he was of the house and lineage of David:) to be taxed with Mary his espoused wife, being great with child." (Luke 2:1, 3–5.)

Bethlehem. The city of David. Ancient homeland of Israel's greatest king. In Hebrew it is called Beth Lechem, which literally means "The House of Bread."[7] How perfect that He who was to take the throne of David and become Israel's ultimate king should come to earth in the city of His illustrious ancestor! How fitting that He who would be known as the "Bread of Life" should enter mortality in the tiny village called "The House of Bread." (See John 6:35.)

Though His birth is celebrated in December, latter-day revelation explains that it actually occurred in the spring. (See D&C 20:1.)[8] The time would have been late March or early April when Joseph moved

southward with Mary at his side, heavy with the living treasure in her womb. Spring is a time of glorious beauty in Israel. The "latter rains" water the parched soil, and in gratitude the earth responds with an explosion of grass and wildflowers. New life springs from the old with the wildest abundance. What better season to welcome him who would be called the "Prince of life"? (See Acts 3:15.)

SEARCH FOR LODGINGS

"And so it was, that, while they were there, the days were accomplished that she should be delivered. And she brought forth her firstborn son, and wrapped him in swaddling clothes, and laid him in a manger; because there was no room for them in the inn." (Luke 2:6–7.)

No room in the inn. If, as we believe, it was April and not December, then it was very likely Passover season in Jerusalem. This could explain the reason Joseph took Mary on the rigorous, sixty-mile journey to Judea when she was in the final month of her pregnancy. The Roman "taxing" mentioned by Luke was more accurately a census or enrollment. Each family head had to register and give an accounting of his property so that taxes could be levied. But while there was considerable flexibility in timing allowed to meet this requirement, if it was Passover season when they went, they would be able to meet their religious responsibilities as well. The Mosaic law required that every adult male bring his sacrifices before the Lord (i.e., to the temple) each year at Passover. (See Exodus 23:14–19.) So, by choosing this time of year, Joseph could fulfill both requirements.

Today we can hardly conceive of the magnitude of this most important of all Jewish festivals. From all over the empire, Jews returned to their homeland at Passover. Though determining exactly how large Jerusalem was during this period is difficult, the population was probably between one and two hundred thousand. Josephus tells us that during Passover "innumerable multitudes came thither [to Jerusalem] out of the country."[9] In another place, he was more specific. Because the Paschal Lamb had to be totally consumed by the family in the ritual meal (See Exodus 12:10), tradition stated that no fewer than ten and no more than twenty could gather for each lamb sacrificed. Josephus tells us that during one Passover of his time (about a.d. 70), 256,500 lambs were sacrificed.[10] Even using the more conservative figure of ten, that still means the population of Jerusalem at Passover had swollen by more than 1,000 percent to the staggering number of nearly three million people.

The throngs must have been incredible, the facilities throughout the city taxed beyond belief. And with Bethlehem only six miles south of Jerusalem, no wonder there was no room at the inn. Luke probably could have said with equal accuracy, "There was no room anywhere."

Often in the art and literature surrounding the Christmas story, the unnamed innkeeper of the scriptural account is viewed as selfish and uncaring, an insensitive oaf unmoved by the plight of a woman heavy with child. This may make for interesting art and literature, but it is not justified by the scriptural record. In the first place, the "inns" of the ancient Middle East were not quaint and homey little buildings with thatched roofs and latticed windows from which warm lamplight beckoned the weary traveler. The inns of the Holy Land were typically large, fortress-like buildings, built around a spacious open square. Called *khans* or *caravanserai*, they provided stopping places for the caravans of the ancient world.

Just as modern hotels and motels must provide parking for automobiles, so did a *caravanserai* have to provide a place where the donkeys, camels, and other animals could be safely cared for. Inside the *khan*, which was usually of two-story construction, all the "rooms" faced the courtyard. They were typically arched, open antechambers facing out onto the square. Here the traveler could build a small fire or sleep within clear view of his animals and goods. "In these hostelries, bazaars and markets were held, animals killed and meat sold, also wine and cider; so that they were a much more public place of resort than might at first be imagined."[11]

Even if there had been room at the inn, a *caravanserai* was hardly the ideal place for a woman in labor. Perhaps the innkeeper, moved with compassion at Mary's plight and knowing of her need and desire for privacy, offered them his stable. Perhaps Joseph found the place on his own. The scriptures do not say. But one thing is very probable and contradicts another popular misconception: the birth likely did not take place in a wooden shed with pitched roof as is so commonly depicted in nativity scenes around the world.

In Bethlehem today stands the Church of the Nativity. Beneath the church is a large grotto or cave. In southern Judea, including the area around Bethlehem, limestone caves are common. Such caves provided natural shelter for the flocks and herds of ancient Israel. They were warm, protected from inclement weather, and could easily be blocked to keep the animals safe for the night. The tradition that this grotto was the stable of Luke's account is very old and accepted by many scholars. President Harold B. Lee, then of the Quorum of the Twelve, visited this grotto in 1958 and confirmed that in his mind it was "a hallowed spot, . . . a sacred place."[12]

So, there in the sheltered warmth of a cave, beneath the limestone hills of Bethlehem, He who was to become the Good Shepherd—not of the sheep that grazed the hills of Israel, but of the human flock—was born and cradled in a manger.

That seems almost beyond our comprehension. Here was Jesus—a member of the Godhead, the Firstborn of the Father, the Creator, Jehovah of the Old Testament—leaving His divine and holy station, divesting Himself of all that glory and majesty to enter the body of a tiny infant: helpless, completely dependent on His mother and earthly "father." That He should come to a lowly stable and not to the finest of earthly palaces and be swaddled in purple and showered with jewels is astonishing. Little wonder that the angel said to Nephi, "Behold the condescension of God!" (1 Nephi 11:26.)

ANNOUNCEMENT TO THE SHEPHERDS

"And there were in the same country shepherds abiding in the field, keeping watch over their flock by night. And, lo, the angel of the Lord came upon them, and the glory of the Lord shone round about them: and they were sore afraid. And the angel said unto them, Fear not: for, behold, I bring you good tidings of great joy, which shall be to all people. For unto you is born this day in the city of David a Saviour, which is Christ the Lord. And this shall be a sign unto you; Ye shall find the babe wrapped in swaddling clothes, lying in a manger." (Luke 2:8–12.)

One of these verses is frequently misquoted: "Keeping watch over their flocks by night." But the verse does not say flocks (plural) but flock (singular). One scholar explained the significance: "There was near Bethlehem, on the road to Jerusalem, a tower known as Migdal Eder, or the watchtower of the flock. Here was the station where shepherds watched the flocks destined for sacrifice in the temple. . . . It was a settled conviction among the Jews that the Messiah was to be born in Bethlehem, and equally that he was to be revealed from Migdal Eder. The beautiful significance of the revelation of the infant Christ

to shepherds watching the flocks destined for sacrifice needs no comment."[13]

Sometimes in translation the power of the original language is considerably lessened. While the words, in English, of the angel to the shepherds are beautiful and significant, we miss much of the electrifying impact the original words must have had on those men of Judea. Let us examine just two or three of the phrases given to the shepherds that night, assuming they were given in Aramaic.

"*In the city of David.*" We have already seen that the Jews expected Bethlehem to be the birthplace of the Messiah. This in part stemmed from the prophet Micah, who centuries before had specified the place. (See Micah 5:2.)

"*Is born a Savior.*" The word that meant "Savior" was Yeshua. In the Greek New Testament that name was transliterated into *Hee-ay-sous,* or, in English, "Jesus." When the angel announced to Joseph that Mary would bear a son, note what he said: "Thou shalt call his name Jesus [*Yeshua*]: for he shall *save* his people from their sins." (Matthew 1:21, emphasis added.)

"*Which is Christ.*" Our English word *Christ* is derived directly from the Greek, *Christos.* It means "the anointed one."[14] *Christos* was a direct translation of the Hebrew word, *Messhiach,* which meant exactly the same thing—the anointed one. *Messhiach* is, of course, transliterated into English as "Messiah."

"The Lord." The simple title "Lord" is perhaps the most significant of all, yet we totally miss its importance in the translation. In the Old Testament the name of God was written with four Hebrew consonants: YHVH. Because vowels were not written in Hebrew, there has been some debate as to its proper pronunciation. Modern scholars often write it as *Yahweh*, but the King James translators wrote it as *Jehovah*.

The Jews of ancient times, however, viewed the name as being so sacred that it should not be pronounced out loud. Whenever they found it written, they would substitute the Hebrew word *adonai*, meaning "my Lord." The translators who produced the King James Version of the Old Testament honored that tradition of the Jews, and where they found the name YHVH, they wrote in (with very few exceptions) "the Lord." However, *adonai* can also be used as a title of respect for men, as in the phrase "My lord, the king." To distinguish between the two uses, the translators wrote *Lord* in small capital letters if it represented the name of deity and regular upper and lower case letters if used normally. (See, for example, 2 Samuel 15:21, where both uses are found in the same verse.) The declaration of the angel to the shepherds used *Lord* or *Adonai* in reference to deity; literally it could be translated Jehovah.

Now we begin to sense the impact of the angel's words upon these shepherds. In essence, here is his pronouncement: "Unto you is born this day in the city prophesied to be the birthplace of the Messiah, *Yeshua* (or Jesus), the Savior, who is the Anointed One (the Messiah), and who is also Jehovah, the God of your fathers."

"And they came with haste, and found Mary, and Joseph, and the babe lying in a manger. And when they had seen it, they made known abroad the saying which was told them concerning this child. And all they that heard it wondered at those things which were told them by the shepherds. But Mary kept all these things, and pondered them in her heart." (Luke 2:16–19.)

1. Alfred Edersheim, *Sketches of Jewish Social Life in the Days of Christ* (Grand Rapids, Mich.: Wm. B. Eerdmans Publishing Co., 1979), 70.

2. See Edersheim, *Sketches of Jewish Social Life*, 105.

3. Ibid., 143–44.

4. See Robert Young, *Analytical Concordance to the Bible* (Grand Rapids, Mich.: Wm. B. Eerdmans, 1972), 647.

5. From D&C 20:1 we learn that the birth date of the Savior was April 6. See also James E. Talmage, *Jesus the Christ*, Classics in Mormon Literature Edition (Salt Lake City: Deseret Book Co., 1982), 96–98 (102–4 earlier editions). Counting nine months backwards puts the time somewhere around July.

6. In Luke 2:24, we are told that Mary and Joseph offered as the required sacrifice for their firstborn son two turtledoves or pigeons. In Leviticus 12:6–8, where the requirement is given, we are told that the sacrifice should be a lamb, but if the family "be not able" (that is, they are financially unable to afford a lamb), they may instead offer the turtledoves or pigeons.

7. See Merrill F. Unger, ed., *Unger's Bible Dictionary*, 3d ed. (Chicago: Moody Press, 1966), 40.

8. See D&C 20:1; see also note 5 above.

9. Flavius Josephus, *The Antiquities of the Jews*, in *Josephus: Complete Works*, trans. William Whiston (Grand Rapids, Mich.: Kregel Publications, 1960), 17.9.3.

10. See Josephus, *Wars of the Jews*, in *Complete Works*, 7.9.3.

11. Unger, *Unger's Bible Dictionary*, 527.

12. Harold B. Lee, "I Walked Today Where Jesus Walked," *BYU Speeches of the Year*, 10 December 1958, 5.

13. M. R. Vincent, *Word Studies in the New Testament* (MacDill AFB, Florida: MacDonald Publishing Company, n.d.), 142.

14. See Unger, *Unger's Bible Dictionary*, 195.